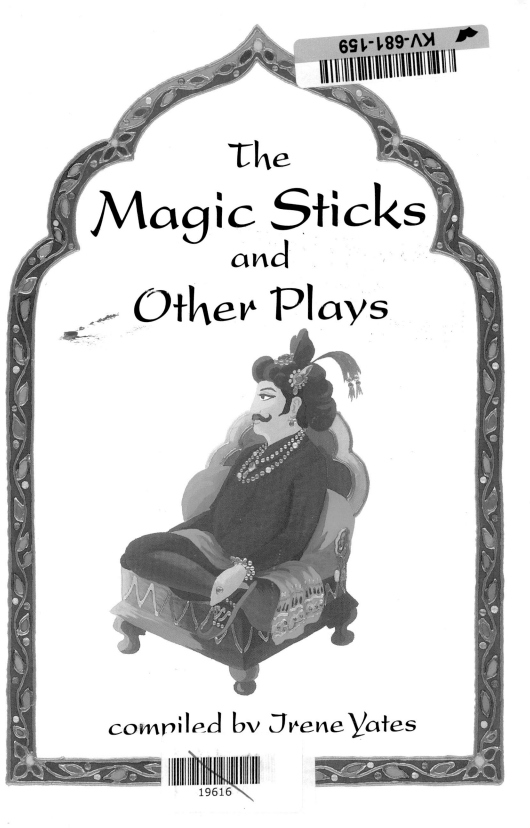

The
Magic Sticks
and
Other Plays

compiled by Irene Yates

Contents

How to Read the Plays............3
Irene Yates

Rumpelstiltskin.....................4
Angela Lanyon

The Magic Sticks..................25
Robina Beckles Willson

Pirates Bold.........................37
Jacquie Buttriss and Ann Callander

How to Read the Plays

The three plays in this book are for you to read aloud in small groups. There are six parts in each play, including the narrator. If your group is smaller than six, the narrator's part could be read by one of the characters.

Follow the play carefully and when it is your turn to speak, remember to say your part clearly. Try to speak the way your character would talk. If you think your character is loud and bossy then you should read the part in a loud, bossy voice. If you are reading the part of a king or somebody very important, try to convey this in the way you read your lines.

1. Skim through the play and look over your parts.

2. Read your lines quietly to yourself.

3. Read the play aloud in your group.

4. Re-read the play and make sure that you use the right sort of voice for your character.

5. Swap roles and read the part of a different character.

Rumpelstiltskin

A Traditional Tale
Retold by Angela Lanyon
Illustrations by Mik Brown

Cast

Narrator

Lisa – a sensible
and thoughtful girl

Mother – a kind but
rather silly person

Father – a rather
foolish boaster

King – a greedy
and selfish man

Rumpelstiltskin (Rumpel-stilts-kin)
– a mysterious magical character

Rumpelstiltskin

Narrator *In a cottage in a village in a small country, Lisa has been baking. Her mother and father are very proud of her. They are always telling people how clever she is and all the wonderful things she can do.*

Mother Oh, Lisa, what lovely things you've made. You're really brilliant. Twenty currant buns, twelve jam tarts, and one apple pie. All fit for a King to eat.

Father When the King comes to the village today, I am going to tell him how clever you are.

Narrator *At that moment there is the sound of cheering outside.*

Mother Quick, Lisa, see if that's the King coming. I hope he visits us so I can show him all the wonderful things you've made.

Narrator *Lisa goes to the window and looks out.*

Lisa Look, the King has stopped at our gate.

Father I bet he can smell all this lovely food! I'm sure the King would want to marry a girl as clever as you.

Narrator *Just then the King puts his head through the window.*

King I can smell apple pie – my favourite.

Mother Oh please, Your Majesty, come and try a slice.

Narrator *The King comes into the cottage. Mother cuts a slice of pie and gives it to him.*

King Scrumptious! Delicious!

Narrator *The King licks his fingers.*

King   That's the best pie I've ever tasted.
Who made it?

Father   My daughter, Lisa made it and she's
the cleverest girl there ever was.

Narrator   *The King starts to move to the door,
but Lisa's mother takes hold of the
King's arm.*

Mother   Now before you rush off…

Father   Yes, do hang on, Your Majesty, and I'll
tell you about Lisa. She can bake the
best pies in the world and she can
weave the most beautiful cloth and
spin the finest thread.

Lisa   Oh Father, please be quiet. I'm sure the
King is in a hurry.

King   There are plenty of people at the
palace who can bake and weave and
spin.

Father   None of them can be as clever as Lisa.
She's so clever she can do anything.
Anything at all.

Lisa   Father, don't be silly.

Mother   Go on, Your Majesty, you ask her.

King   What shall I ask her to do?

Narrator   *While Mother is thinking, Father interrupts.*

Father   I know. Ask her to spin straw into gold.

Lisa   Oh please, Your Majesty, please don't take any notice of Father. Of course I can't spin straw into gold.

Mother   But Lisa, you're so clever, you probably could spin straw into gold if you tried.

Narrator   *Lisa whispers to her mother.*

Lisa   Mother, you know I can't spin straw into gold.

King   It doesn't seem very likely but never mind, we can soon find out. My kingdom's not very rich and I could do with some more gold. You can come back to the palace and if you really can turn straw into gold you'll be well rewarded. But if not, I shall cut off your head.

Narrator   *Lisa starts to cry.*

Lisa   But no one can spin straw into gold, Your Majesty.

Narrator   *Lisa's mother looks worried. She is beginning to regret what she and Lisa's father have told the King.*

Mother   Please, Your Majesty, her father was only joking.

Father   Yes, yes, I was only joking.

Narrator   *The King isn't listening. He looks very stern.*

King   If you're telling the truth, she's nothing to fear. But if not …

Narrator   *Taking hold of Lisa's arm, the King walks out of the cottage.*

Narrator   *It is night. In a room high in a tower, Lisa is crying. There is a spinning wheel beside her and a big heap of straw.*

Lisa   Oh dear, I can't possibly make gold out of straw, and when the King finds out, he'll cut off my head.

Narrator   *Suddenly there is a scratching noise and a strange little man with a long pointed nose climbs through the window.*

10

Rumpelstiltskin Why are you crying?

Lisa Because my father told the King I could spin straw into gold. Now the King will cut off my head.

Narrator *The little man laughs.*

Rumpelstiltskin That's nothing to cry about. I'll help you if you give me something in exchange.

Lisa But I haven't got anything.

Rumpelstiltskin What about that pretty necklace you're wearing?

Lisa This?

Narrator *The little man nods and Lisa unfastens the necklace and hands it to him.*

Rumpelstiltskin That's right. Now you go to sleep. By the time you wake up all your troubles will be over.

Narrator   *In the morning Lisa wakes to find a heap of shining gold instead of the heap of straw. The King comes in.*

King   So your father told the truth. You can spin straw into gold.

Narrator   *Lisa wants to tell the King what has happened but she is so frightened that when she opens her mouth to speak no words come out.*

King   There's no need to be afraid, Lisa. You've kept your word.

Lisa   Can I go home now?

King   Not yet, I need more gold.

Narrator   *The King leads Lisa to another room in the castle. It is even bigger and filled with straw.*

King Tonight you must spin all this straw. But remember... if it isn't turned into gold by tomorrow morning, I'll cut off your head.

Narrator *The King goes away and Lisa is alone. She runs to the window and looks out.*

Lisa Perhaps the little man will come back tonight to help me.

Narrator *That night Lisa hears the scratching noise at the window. The strange little man climbs in through the window.*

Rumpelstiltskin More straw to spin? My favourite task.

Lisa But I have nothing to give you.

Rumpelstiltskin What about that pretty ring you're wearing?

Lisa This?

Narrator *The little man nods and Lisa takes off her ring and hands it to him.*

Rumpelstiltskin It'll do. It'll do. Now go to sleep and in the morning there'll be heaps of gold instead of heaps of straw.

Narrator *In the morning, Lisa opens her eyes and stretches. There is a big pile of gold in the middle of the floor. The King comes in.*

King Well done, Lisa. You have spun more gold.

Lisa Please can I go home now?

King No, now you must come with me.

Narrator *The King leads Lisa to the tower. It is filled with straw.*

King I've had people searching the countryside for every last wisp of straw. If you can spin it all into gold, then I will make you my Queen. But remember ... if it isn't turned into gold by tomorrow morning, I'll cut off your head.

14

Narrator *The King goes away and Lisa sits down and begins to cry.*

Lisa If the little man comes again, I have nothing to give him, and if there's no gold tomorrow the King will cut off my head.

Narrator *Lisa hears some shouting from the street below. She looks out of the window and see her mother and father waving to her. Lisa shouts down to them.*

Lisa Father, why did you tell the King I could spin straw into gold?

Father But you *have* spun straw into gold. We saw the soldiers taking it all away in wheelbarrows.

Narrator *Lisa shakes her head and tells her mother and father about the little man who helped her.*

Lisa But I've nothing left to give him next time.

Mother Tell him you'll give him something when you get home.

Father   Promise him whatever he asks.

Lisa   But what if I can't keep the promise?

Father   Forget about it. Don't worry. You'll be miles away by then.

Lisa   I hope you're right. I don't want to get into more trouble.

Narrator   *That night Lisa sits sadly on the floor hoping to hear the scratching sound at the window. At last she hears the little man climbing through the window.*

Rumpelstiltskin   Dry your tears, Lisa. I will help you, but this will be the last time.

Lisa   But I can't pay you. I've nothing left.

Rumpelstiltskin   Now that's a pity. I don't work for nothing.

Lisa   Perhaps I could pay you after I get home.

Narrator   *The little man puts his head on one side and looks at Lisa.*

Rumpelstiltskin   Perhaps, perhaps.

Lisa   Please help me this one last time. The King said he'll make me the Queen if I turn this straw into gold but if I don't, he'll cut off my head.

Rumpelstiltskin   Perhaps we could make a bargain. Are you any good at keeping promises?

Narrator   *Lisa nods.*

Rumpelstiltskin   Then let's shake hands on it.

Lisa   But what do you want?

Rumpelstiltskin   When you're the Queen, you must give me your first-born child.

Narrator   *Lisa remembers her father's words – 'promise him whatever he asks'.*

Rumpelstiltskin   Is it a bargain?

Lisa   Yes, I promise.

17

Narrator *In the morning the tower is full of gold. The King comes in and claps his hands with delight.*

King Well done, Lisa. I'm going to marry you and you'll be my Queen. You and your mother and father will live in the palace for the rest of your lives.

Narrator *Lisa is so delighted that she forgets all about her promise to the little man.*

Narrator *A year passes and the King and Lisa have a baby son. In the nursery Lisa and her mother and father are playing with the baby. They are bending over the cot when the door springs open. It is the strange little man with the pointed nose.*

Rumpelstiltskin It's time to keep your promise, little Queen.

Lisa What promise?

Rumpelstiltskin Your first-born child. You promised me.

Lisa But that was a long time ago.

Father   This is the King's son. You can't take him away.

Rumpelstiltskin   Oh can't I? Just wait and see.

Lisa   You can have as much gold as you want but leave me my baby.

Narrator   *Lisa picks up the baby and holds him tightly. The little man comes very close.*

Rumpelstiltskin   I've plenty of gold. But I will do you a deal. I have a riddle and if you can answer it within three days, you shall get to keep your son. If not, the baby's mine.

Lisa What's the riddle?

Rumpelstiltskin Just tell me my name. Each day you can have three guesses.

Narrator *Lisa thinks hard.*

Lisa Is it John? Is it Samuel? Could it be Mark?

Narrator *Each time the little man shakes his head. Then he laughs and stamps his feet on the ground and whirls out of the room.*

Lisa Oh, Mother! How can we possibly find out his name? There are thousands to choose from.

Mother Oh, Lisa. It's all our fault. I am sorry.

Narrator *The following day, Lisa is in the nursery holding the baby. The door opens and the little man dances into the room.*

Rumpelstiltskin Well now, have you guessed? Three days and three guesses on each day.

Narrator *The little man laughs but his laugh is cruel.*

Rumpelstiltskin Sit and cuddle your darling son,
For tomorrow you'll have none.
Riddles and tricks are my game
You won't ever guess my name.

Lisa Is it William?

Mother It must be Jonathan.

Father I bet it's something right out of the
ordinary. Marmaduke!

Rumpelstiltskin Wrong every time. And don't forget.
You've only got until tomorrow and
then the baby's mine.

Narrator *The little man whirls away,*
cackling with laughter.

Lisa What can I do?
How can I stop him?

Mother Leave it to Father
and me. We'll
follow him. He
can't have gone
far.

Narrator *It's dark and Mother and Father are in the woods. They have followed the little man. Mother hides behind a bush. Someone is singing. She sees the little man dancing around a small fire. Father creeps nearer.*

Rumpelstiltskin Wife and family I have none,
But tomorrow I'll have the King's own son.
Tricks and riddles are my game,
Rumpelstiltskin is my name.

Narrator *Mother and Father creep away without making a sound.*

Narrator *The following day, in the nursery, Lisa holds the baby. She and her mother and father wait for the little man to come back. The door flies open and the little man enters. He is grinning.*

Rumpelstiltskin Now then, little Queen. You have three guesses left.

Father I bet it's Jason.

Mother Is it Oliver?

Narrator *The little man laughs and reaches out to take the baby. Lisa shouts.*

Lisa I know! It's Rumpelstiltskin!

Narrator *The little man gives a great cry of rage and stamps his feet.*

Rumpelstiltskin You cheated. You cheated. You must have cheated!

Lisa Go away, Rumpelstiltskin and leave us alone. Don't ever come back.

Narrator *Rumpelstiltskin looks at Lisa and Mother. Then he looks at Father. Then he stamps so hard on the floor that his foot goes right through it. He is so angry that he vanishes in a puff of smoke.*

Lisa   And now my baby's safe. Oh, Mother, Father, how ever can I thank you?

Mother   You don't need to thank us. If it wasn't for us, you wouldn't have been in this mess.

Father   Yes we've learnt our lesson. We'll never boast about you again – even if you are the best daughter in the world and we've got the very best little grandson.

Do you think that Lisa's father has really learnt a lesson?

Do you think Lisa and the King will live happily ever after?

The
Magic Sticks

A Traditional Tale
Retold by Robina Beckles Willson
Illustrations by Kiran Ahmad

Cast

Narrator   **Judge** – a fair and just man   **Guard** – a faithful servant

King – a wise and clever ruler

Jaspal   two women who have been accused of stealing   **Sita**

The Magic Sticks

Narrator *Long ago, there was a King who lived in India. Every morning he sat on a throne in his golden palace and people came to ask him for advice. One day, a judge came to ask the King for help.*

Guard The judge is here to see you, Your Highness.

Judge Your Highness, you are known to be the wisest King in India. I have come to ask for your help with a most difficult case in my law court.

King I will do what I can. Tell me more.

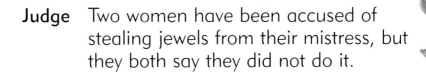

Judge Two women have been accused of stealing jewels from their mistress, but they both say they did not do it.

King Then it is quite simple. You need to find out who is telling the truth.

Judge That is not easy, Your Highness. They both talk so much and tell such good stories, I don't know who to believe.

King Then how can I help?

Judge Please would you ask them some questions for me?

King I will see what I can do. Where are the women now? What are their names?

Judge They are at the law court, and they are called Jaspal and Sita.

King Then I shall send an elephant to bring them here. Guard?

Guard Yes, Your Highness.

King Take my elephant and bring back Jaspal and Sita.

Guard Yes, Your Highness. I will bring them with all speed.

Narrator *Soon the two women arrive at the palace and come in to the King's throne room.*

Guard Here are Jaspal and Sita, Your Highness.

King   Thank you, Guard. Wait here. I may need you. Now, which of you two is Jaspal?

Jaspal   I am Jaspal, Your Highness.

King   I believe some jewels were stolen from your mistress.

Jaspal   Yes, Your Highness.

King   Did you steal them from her?

Jaspal   No, Your Highness.

King   Tell me your story. Where were you when you heard the jewels were missing?

Jaspal   I had just arrived at my mistress' house for work. She was sitting in her bedroom, crying and holding her empty jewel box.

King   When did you last see the jewels?

Jaspal   The night before. It was my turn to help my mistress to get dressed for a party. I did her hair and gave her the jewels she asked for.

King   What jewels did she wear?

Jaspal   A diamond tiara for her hair, a diamond ring and a necklace of gold elephants.

King   And when your mistress was ready for the party, where did she put the jewellery box?

Jaspal   In a locked treasure chest.

King   And where did she put the key?

Jaspal   I don't know, Your Highness. She has never told me where the key is kept.

Sita   Of course not! She wouldn't trust you.

Judge   Silence until the King asks you to speak.

King   Very well, Sita. And when did you last see your mistress' jewels?

Sita   I live at my mistress' house and wouldn't dream of stealing a grain of rice from her. I saw the jewels the day before they were stolen. My mistress asked me to clean some silver bangles for her. I sat in her bedroom and cleaned them all. There were twenty silver bangles.

King   And did your mistress count them when she put them back in the box?

Sita   Of course not. She trusts me.

King   I have heard enough. Guard, take them outside.

Guard   At once, Your Highness.

Judge   So who is the thief, Your Highness?

King   I can't tell you now, but I'll be able to tell you in the morning. Guard, bring in Jaspal and Sita again and bring me my box with the magic sticks.

Guard   Very well, Your Highness.

Narrator   *As Jaspal and Sita come back into the room the guard hands the box to the King. The King takes out two sticks and holds them up in front of Jaspal and Sita.*

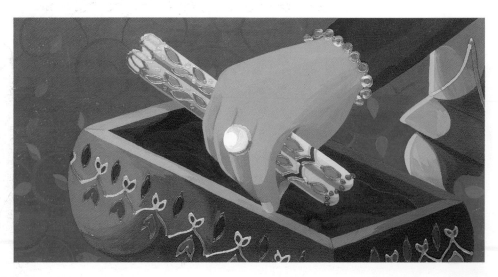

King   Jaspal and Sita, I am going to give each of you a magic stick. As you can see, the two sticks look exactly the same but, because they are magic, one of the sticks will grow in the night. Whoever has that stick is the thief. Guard, take them to their rooms, then bring them back here in the morning.

Guard   I will, Your Highness.

Narrator   *All night long, the judge wondered who was the thief – Jaspal or Sita.*
The next morning, the King went to his throne room. The judge watched as Jaspal and Sita were brought into the throne room to hand their magic sticks to the King.

Guard   Here are Jaspal and Sita, Your Highness.

King   Now. Last night these two magic sticks were the same size. In my right hand I have Jaspal's stick. In my left hand I have Sita's stick. Look at them now.

Judge   Sita's stick is shorter! You said that whoever had the stick that grew would be the thief. Jaspal must be the thief!

King   No. Sita is the thief.

Judge   How can that be?

King   I said that the sticks were magic – but they were not. Sita knew she had stolen the jewels and thought that her stick would grow in the night. So she cut a piece off. Now it is the shorter stick.

Sita   I've been tricked!

King   Jaspal, you may go free. You told the truth. You did not steal the jewels. Guard, take Jaspal back to her mistress' house.

Guard   Yes, Your Highness.

King   You, Sita, will be sent to prison. But first you must tell the judge the whole story.

Judge   Thank you, Your Highness. You *are* the wisest King in India!

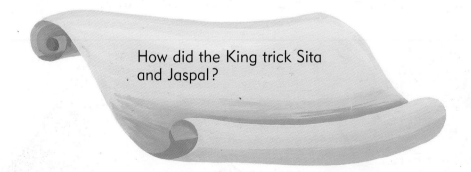

How did the King trick Sita and Jaspal?

Pirates Bold

A Fantasy Play
by Jacquie Buttriss and Ann Callander
Illustrations by Toni Goffe

Cast

Narrator

Captain Cod – a cowardly sea captain

Pepper – a sailor who always tries to please her captain

Salt – a nervous sailor

Vinegar – the ship's cook

Chips – the captain's parrot

Pirates Bold

Narrator *Captain Cod and his crew, Salt, Pepper, Vinegar and Chips the parrot, are sailing their ship, 'The Battered Sole'. They are looking for Boot Island where Redbeard the pirate has hidden his treasure.*

Salt Land ahoy!

Pepper Island in sight, Captain.

Captain Cod Aha, we are there at last.

Salt But where are we?

Pepper We're here.

Salt But where is here?

Captain Cod Fetch the map.

Salt Aye, aye, Captain.

Chips Aye, aye, Captain. Give us a kiss!

Pepper Pesky parrot.

Narrator *Salt goes to fetch the map.*

Captain Cod I'm hungry. What's for tea, Vinegar?

Chips Cod and chips! Cod and chips!

Captain Cod Pesky parrot.

Vinegar Well, Captain. There's fish on toast, or toast on fish.

Captain Cod That sounds yummy. I'll have…

Narrator *But just then Salt comes running up to the captain.*

Salt   Here is the map, Captain.

Pepper   What are we looking for?

Captain Cod   Redbeard's treasure. He buried it on Boot Island, just…here.

Narrator   *Captain Cod points to a cross on the map.*

Salt   Why is it called Boot Island?

Pepper   It doesn't look like a boot to me.

Captain Cod   The Captain looks puzzled.

Vinegar   That's because you've got the map the wrong way up, Captain.

Chips   Who's a clever boy, then?

Captain Cod   Pesky parrot.

Narrator *Suddenly, Salt calls out…*

Salt We're nearing land, Captain.

Captain Cod Look through the telescope, Pepper. See if it's safe to go ashore.

Pepper Aye, aye, Captain.

Chips Aye, aye, Captain. Give us a kiss!

Captain Cod Pesky parrot.

Narrator *Pepper looks through the telescope.*

Captain Cod What can you see?

Pepper Steep, craggy cliffs, Captain…and huge, jagged rocks in the sea.

Captain Cod Oh dear, we can't land here…it's much too frightening for me.

Chips Who's a brave boy, then?

Captain Cod Just you be quiet, pesky parrot. Anyway, I'm still hungry. Where's my tea?

Chips Up the crow's nest! Up the crow's nest!

Vinegar Pesky parrot. Here's your tea, Captain. Fish on toast.

Narrator *The Captain tucks in while the crew sail the ship.*

Pepper What's for *our* tea?

Salt Not fish, I hope.

Vinegar Yes, fish or toast.

Pepper Toast sounds yummy.

Salt We'll have toast on toast.

Narrator	*After tea the crew sail the ship round the island. The Captain gives the telescope to Pepper.*
Captain Cod	Take a look here, Pepper. Can you see any cliffs?
Pepper	No, Captain. Just a sandy beach.
Captain Cod	Good. Can you see any rocks, Salt?
Salt	No rocks in sight, Captain.
Captain Cod	Aha! This place will do then. Prepare to land, shipmates.
Salt & Pepper	Aye, aye, Captain.
Chips	Aye, aye, Captain. Put the kettle on.
Pepper	Pesky parrot. Get out of the way.
Captain Cod	Have we got time for a little snack?
Vinegar	Yes, Captain. You can have fish fingers, fish burgers or fish stew.
Captain Cod	That sounds yummy. Give me lots of fish fingers.

Narrator *The Captain tucks in while the crew get ready to land. Soon the pirates are ready to set off and explore the island.*

Pepper We could climb that hill, Captain…

Salt …and see what's on the other side.

Captain Cod Good thinking, shipmates. Now, I'm the Captain so…you go first. I'll just rest here for a while.

Chips Who's a brave boy, then?

Captain Cod Pesky parrot.

Narrator *Salt, Pepper and Vinegar climb to the top of the steep hill.*

Pepper Look.

Narrator *Salt and Vinegar, in turn, look through the telescope.*

Salt Oh dear. The Captain's not going to like this.

Vinegar We will have to tell him though.

Narrator *The crew go back to see the Captain.*

Captain Cod Well, what did you see?

Salt	There was a steep, rocky path…
Pepper	…then a wide, green valley…
Vinegar	…with a river running through it.
Captain Cod	Aha!
Salt	But…tell him, Pepper.
Captain Cod	Tell me what?
Pepper	Beyond the river, Captain, there's a jungle.
Vinegar	A deep, dark jungle that stretches across the island and seems to have no end.
Captain Cod	Oh dear, we can't go that way… jungles are much too frightening for me.
Chips	Who's a brave boy, then?
Captain Cod	Pesky parrot.
Narrator	*They all go back to the ship and set sail again.*
Pepper	Where shall we go now, Captain?

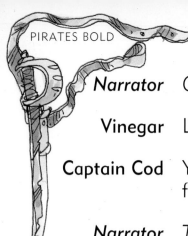

Narrator *Captain Cod looks at the map.*

Vinegar Let's sail to Crazy Creek.

Captain Cod Yes, good thinking, Vinegar. We might find some fish to catch.

Narrator *The pirates sail on towards Crazy Creek.*

Captain Cod Look through the telescope, Pepper. What can you see?

Pepper I can see a swamp, Captain.

Captain Cod Is it safe?

Vinegar Probably, if we keep to the path.

Narrator *The pirates land and they all step ashore.*

Captain Cod Well, I'm the Captain so … you lead the way.

Chips Aye, aye, Captain. Give us a kiss!

Captain Cod Pesky parrot.

Narrator *They follow the long, winding path through the swamp.*

Captain Cod I'm tired. I'll have to sit down on this log.

Salt It can't be far now, Captain.

Pepper We'll soon have Redbeard's treasure.

Captain Cod I'm hungry. Have we got any cakes?

Vinegar Fish cakes, Captain.

Captain Cod That will do nicely.

Narrator *The Captain sits on the log and tucks into the fish cakes.*

Vinegar I wonder what Redbeard's treasure is?

Chips Cod and Chips.

Captain Cod Pesky parrot.

Narrator *Suddenly, the crew step back.*

Pepper C-C-C-Captain … that log has eyes …

Salt … and an enormous mouth

Vinegar … and sharp t-t-teeth.

Narrator *The crew turn and start to run away.*

Captain Cod Help! It's a pirate-eating crocodile. Wait for me!

Narrator   *As Captain Cod runs to catch up with the others, the crocodile snaps its jaws and rips off the seat of his trousers.*

Captain Cod   Help! Help! I'm being eaten alive… save me… this is MUCH too frightening for me!

Chips   Who's a brave boy, then?

Narrator   *The pirates hurry back and are safe on board the ship.*

Captain Cod   That was frightening. I need something to eat.

Vinegar   I'll go and make a nice fish pie, Captain.

Narrator   *Meanwhile, Salt and Pepper both look at the map.*

Salt   Where shall we go now?

Chips   Up the crow's nest! Up the crow's nest!

Pepper   Pesky parrot. There's only one place left to land, Captain.

Salt   Palm Beach.

Captain Cod   That sounds like a good place to land.

Narrator   *The pirates sail to the top of the island and land on Palm Beach.*

Pepper   Look at all the palm trees.

Captain Cod   Can you see any bananas?

Vinegar   I don't think these trees grow bananas, Captain.

Chips   Who's a silly boy, then?

Captain Cod   Pesky parrot. Well, we had better move on then.

Narrator   *The pirates walk up the beach and through the trees. They walk up to the top of a hill.*

Salt   Captain, look below!

Pepper   We're right on top of a cliff.

Salt   And I can see a river down below.

Captain Cod   I don't like looking down. This is much too frightening for me!

Chips   Who's a brave boy, then?

Narrator   *Suddenly, Vinegar spies something moving in the distance.*

Vinegar   Look. There's a bridge over there.

Salt   We can use it to get across.

Captain Cod   But it's … it's … swaying. It's swaying from side to side.

Vinegar   Yes, it's a rope bridge.

Captain Cod   It doesn't look very safe to me.

Salt   But we'll have to cross it if we want to find the treasure.

Captain Cod   Well, I'm the Captain so…you go and find the treasure.

Chips   Who's a brave boy then?

Captain Cod   Pesky parrot.

Pepper   Yes, Captain. You stay here and have something to eat while we look for the treasure.

Vinegar   Would you like some fish sandwiches?

Captain Cod   That will do nicely.

Narrator   *The crew leave the Captain and go off to find the treasure. They make their way across the swaying bridge.*

Salt   Which way now?

Pepper Let's go this way.

Narrator *The three pirates follow the map until they come to some stones on the ground.*

Salt What a lot of stones!

Pepper It looks like somebody has put them here.

Vinegar This must be where the treasure is.

Salt How do you know?

Vinegar Look at the stones. Look at the shape they make.

Pepper Oh yes. It looks like a cross.

Vinegar It's like the cross on the map.

Salt Let's dig here.

Narrator *The pirates lift off some of the rocks and dig a deep hole in the middle of the cross.*

Pepper Look. There's something metal.

Salt   It's a chest.

Vinegar   It must be Redbeard's treasure!

Narrator   *The pirates carry the chest back to the bridge. Then they put it down.*

Salt   Phew! It's too heavy.

Vinegar   Yes, it's heavy. But we'll have to get the chest across the bridge somehow.

Narrator   *They all pick up the chest and walk on to the bridge. The bridge sways from side to side.*

Pepper   Help! What's happening?

Salt   The bridge has gone all wobbly.

Vinegar   Look at that rope. It's going to snap.

Salt   What shall we do?

Pepper   Let's make a run for it.

Narrator   *The three pirates hurry across to the other side with the chest.*

Salt   One more step…

Narrator   *Just then the rope snaps.*

Pepper Quick! Jump for it.

Narrator *The three pirates jump, just in time.*

Salt Phew! We nearly didn't make it!

Vinegar There goes the bridge.

Narrator *The pirates watch as the bridge falls.*

Salt This treasure had better be worth all this hard work.

Narrator *The pirates make their way back to Captain Cod.*

Captain Cod Well done, shipmates. I knew you would find the treasure.

Chips Who's a clever boy then?

Salt Let's open it, Captain.

Captain Cod I'm the Captain, so … I'll open it.

Narrator *Captain Cod lifts up the lid of the chest and smiles.*

Salt Is there lots of treasure, Captain?

Captain Cod Oh, yes.

Pepper Is there enough for all of us?

Captain Cod Oh, yes.

Salt
Pepper Well, show us, Captain!
Vinegar

Narrator *Captain Cod holds up a tin in each hand.*

Pepper What is it, Captain?

Salt Gold?

Chips Pieces of eight, pieces of eight!

Captain Cod   Keep your beak out of it, you pesky parrot! This is much better than gold. It's fish!

Salt
Pepper   Oh no! Not more fish!
Vinegar

Captain Cod   Yes, fish! My favourite! Come on, shipmates. I'm hungry. Let's eat!

What adventures do the pirates have on the island?

Was Captain Cod a good captain?